Nervous About Nothing

Conquer Anxiety, Master Your Mind, and Transform Your Life with Proven Strategies for Lasting Peace and Resilience

By

Sarah Evans

Table of contents

Introduction

"Nervous About Nothing:" welcomes you! Transform your life, conquer anxiety, and master your mind. In the maze of the human psyche, where contemplations weave many-sided examples and feelings make a perplexing embroidery, this guide is your reference point of light.

As we leave on this extraordinary excursion together, plan to disentangle the strings of tension, figure out the subtleties of your psyche, and saddle the force of insight to shape an existence of enduring harmony and strength.

A. Welcome to the Brain Maze:

In the buzzing of our day to day routines, the brain frequently turns into a labyrinth, loaded up with exciting bends in the road that leave us feeling lost and confused. " Nervous About Nothing" warmly welcomes you and encourages you to bravely and with curiosity explore this intricate maze.

This book isn't simply an aide; It helps you navigate the complexities of your own mind and serves as a companion.

In these pages, you'll find a guide to grasping the internal operations of your cerebrum, unraveling the language of tension, and opening the key to a more settled, stronger you.

The psyche labyrinth might appear to be overwhelming, yet with the right instruments and experiences, it changes into a material where you have the ability to portray serenity.

B. Untangling the Weavings of Anxiety:

Nervousness, similar to strings woven into the texture of our viewpoints, can make unpredictable examples that direct our feelings and activities. The book's dedicated unraveling—a careful examination of these threads to comprehend their origin, nature, and impact on our well-being—takes place in this section.

We deconstruct the anatomy of anxiety into its component parts and shed light on the intricate relationship between hormones and neurotransmitters.

However, this is not simply an academic investigation; it's a viable manual for destroying the bunches of uneasiness that might have taken home in your psyche. Mental mutilations, those unobtrusive contortions in discernment, are analyzed, permitting you to perceive and rethink them actually.

In this unraveling process, anxiety is not completely eliminated; rather, it is transformed into a manageable force and a tool for personal growth and resilience.

C. The Force of Perception:

Insight is the focal point through which we view the world, forming our encounters and impacting our close to home reactions. In "Nervous About Nothing," we shed light on the power of perception and demonstrate how even minute changes in how you perceive the world can have significant effects on your mental health.

This isn't tied in with wearing rose-shaded glasses; it's tied in with fostering a nuanced comprehension of your viewpoints and feelings.

When used with care, perception can transform fears into stepping stones and obstacles into opportunities. You will discover the capacity to navigate the complexities of life with grace and resilience if you accept the transformative potential of your perspective. This section of the book gives you the tools to develop a positive and realistic outlook, laying the groundwork for long-term change in your perception of the world.

As you venture through these central parts of "Nervous About Nothing," imagine this book as a confided in guide, driving you through the brain labyrinth, disentangling uneasiness' strings, and enlightening the unprecedented power inside your discernment.

Together, we leave on a journey for self-revelation and strengthening, where each page carries you more like a daily existence where you are genuinely "Nervous About Nothing."

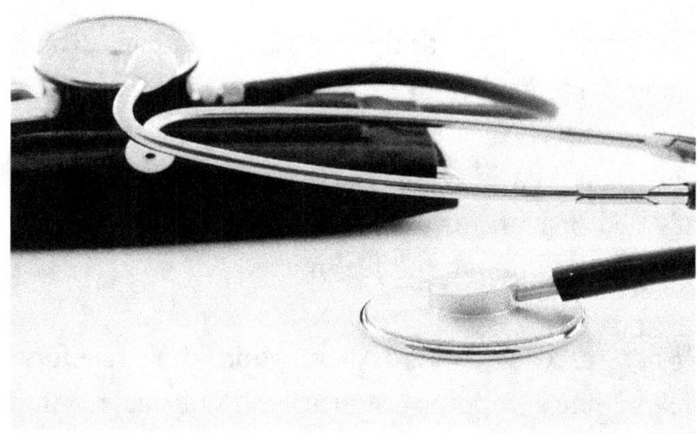

Section one : The Anatomy of Anxiety

In the complex mental landscape, anxiety can appear as a gloomy maze that affects one's thoughts, feelings, and actions. We embark on a journey to comprehend the anatomy of anxiety—a deep dive into the inner workings of the brain, the intricate dance of neurotransmitters, and the subtle choreography of hormones—in order to successfully navigate this maze.

The first chapter of "Nervous About Nothing" serves as your guide throughout this investigation, providing information that enables you to eliminate the causes of anxiety and regain control over your mental health.

A. Dissecting the Mind:

The mind, the war room of our being, assumes an essential part in the embroidery of uneasiness. " Nervous About Nothing" starts by separating the cerebrum, demystifying its intricacy to uncover the locales and organizations that arrange our reactions to the world. We investigate the amygdala, the sentinel of feelings, and the prefrontal cortex, the expert controller of independent direction.

Understanding the perplexing trap of brain associations gives a guide to perceiving how nervousness flourishes. From the limbic framework's personal handling to the mental control habitats, we divulge the associations that shape our reactions to stressors. You gain a new awareness—a compass to navigate the terrain of your thoughts and emotions—as we unravel the intricacies of the brain.

B. Exposing the Neurotransmitters' Hidden Faces:

The mind's messengers, neurotransmitters, are the threads that make up our mental state. Nervous About Nothing" welcomes you in the background to expose these synapses, revealing insight into how they impact nervousness.

Serotonin, the temperament stabilizer; dopamine, the prize framework orchestrator; furthermore, GABA, the quieting guide — each assumes a vital part in molding our close to home scene.

You can gain insight into the factors that can tip the scales in your favor of anxiety by comprehending the delicate balance of neurotransmitters. You can use the tools in this section to support your mental health by learning practical ways to maintain neurotransmitter balance. You can harmonize your brain's symphony of neurotransmitters by making lifestyle changes or practicing mindfulness.

C. The Hormonal Dance:

Past synapses, chemicals play out an expressive dance inside our bodies, impacting temperament, stress reaction, and generally speaking emotional well-being. " The dynamic interaction of cortisol, adrenaline, and oxytocin in "Nervous About Nothing" sheds light on the hormone dance.

These chemicals, when in balance, add to a condition of harmony; be that as it may, irregular characteristics can shift the scale towards increased tension.

You will learn how to recognize the symptoms of hormonal imbalances and how to restore harmony in this section. From way of life changes to pressure the board procedures, you'll figure out how to enhance your hormonal dance for a more settled and stronger psyche. "Nervous About Nothing" gives you the knowledge to create a supportive environment for mental well-being by demystifying the role hormones play in anxiety.

As you dig into Section One, imagine "Nervous About Nothing" as a key opening the secrets of nervousness' underlying foundations. Separating the mind, exposing synapses, and investigating the dance of chemicals lay the preparation for your groundbreaking process.

Outfitted with this comprehension, you're ready to explore the psyche's mind boggling scene and establish the groundwork for a strong and tension free future.

Section Two: Navigating the Thought Landscape

Welcome to the heart of "Nervous About Nothing," where we begin a profound investigation of the thought landscape—the intricate terrain where perceptions are formed, emotions are shaped, and anxiety gains a foothold—into which we are transported.

Section Two is your manual for exploring this intricate domain, offering apparatuses to tame the consistently dynamic monkey mind, unravel mental mutilations, and embrace the extraordinary force of care.

A. Subduing the Monkey Brain:

In the racket of our viewpoints, the monkey mind swings from one branch to another, seldom settling. " Anxious About Nothing" acquaints you with the specialty of subduing this fretful psyche, giving strategies to recapture command over your viewpoints. By understanding the idea of the monkey mind — its propensity to hop from one concern to another — you'll reveal down to earth systems to carry tranquility to the turmoil.

Care works out, breathwork, and mental apparatuses become your partners in this undertaking. Learn to focus on the here and now and let go of the grip of overactive thoughts.

Subduing the monkey mind isn't tied in with wiping out contemplations; It's about creating a mental state that is both balanced and focused. This segment furnishes you with the abilities to be the expert, not the worker, of your own contemplations.

B. Defining Cognitive Irregularities:

Thoughts are powerful builders of our reality, but distorted thoughts can create an anxiety-inducing false narrative. "Nervous About Nothing" walks you through the process of decoding cognitive distortions, which are the subtle misinterpretations that sway how we perceive things.

By perceiving examples like highly contrasting reasoning, catastrophizing, or personalization, you gain the capacity to challenge and reevaluate misshaped considerations.

This section gives a tool stash to mental rebuilding, engaging you to change negative idea designs into additional reasonable and sensible viewpoints. You will acquire the skills to reshape your thought landscape and develop a keen awareness of distorted thinking through real-world examples and practical exercises.

The scaffolding that anxiety relies on is dismantled as you decode these distortions, paving the way for a mindset that is more grounded and resilient.

C. Taking Mindfulness Seriously:

At the center of exploring the ideal scene is the extraordinary act of care. " Nervous About Nothing" welcomes you to embrace care as a useful asset for developing an elevated consciousness of your viewpoints, feelings, and sensations.

Through care, you'll foster a non-critical and tolerating position toward your inward encounters, encouraging a feeling of quiet and presence.

Investigate care reflection, body examine methods, and careful breathing activities intended to moor you right now. This segment goes past hypothesis, offering down to earth direction to flawlessly coordinate care into your regular routine. As you embrace care, you develop a psychological safe-haven — a space where nervousness battles to flourish.

In Section Two, "Nervous About Nothing" turns into your sidekick in exploring the idea scene. Subduing the monkey mind, deciphering mental mutilations, and embracing care are not simple ideas but rather significant techniques that engage you to shape a strong and uneasily safe outlook.

As you dig into these groundbreaking practices, imagine a future where your contemplations become partners on the excursion to enduring harmony and prosperity.

Section Three: Investigation of the dynamic scene

Welcome to the heart of your emotional journey within "Nervous About Nothing," Emotions Unleashed. Section Three is an investigation of the dynamic scene of feelings — a landscape where the rollercoaster ride of sentiments unfurls, making swells that touch each part of our lives.

The emotional rollercoaster, the ripple effect of our emotions, and the transformative art of emotional alchemy are the topics covered in this chapter.

A. Climbing the Emotional Hill:

Feelings are the distinctive tones that paint the material of our lives, yet exploring the close to home rollercoaster can be an exhilarating yet testing experience. " Nervous About Nothing" welcomes you to investigate the subtleties of this rollercoaster ride, giving bits of knowledge into the recurring pattern of feelings.

Understanding the rhythm of your emotions—from highs of happiness to lows of despair—is essential for developing emotional resilience.

This part of the book guides you through methods to ride the profound rollercoaster with elegance. You'll learn to effectively navigate the intensity of emotions rather than being swept away by them.

Close to home mindfulness and guideline become your partners, empowering you to outfit the energy of feelings for self-awareness and prosperity.

B. Recognizing the Effect of the Ripple:

Like pebbles dropped into a pond, emotions cause ripples that last far longer than the initial splash. Nervous About Nothing" enlightens the expanding influence of feelings, showing what your inward close to home scene means for your prosperity as well as your communications with others.

By understanding this interconnected web, you gain knowledge of the significant effect feelings can have on connections, work, and by and large life fulfillment.

The concept of emotional intelligence—the capacity to recognize, comprehend, and control one's own emotions as well as to empathize with those around you—is the focus of this chapter. Functional activities and certifiable models guide you in creating the capacity to appreciate people at their core, improving your capacity to explore social elements and assemble significant associations. As you handle the expanding influence, you gain the devices to make positive floods of progress in your life and the existence of everyone around you.

C. Emotional Transformation:

The transformative process of transforming difficult emotions into sources of strength and wisdom is referred to as emotional alchemy. Nervous About Nothing" acquaints you with the craft of close to home speculative chemistry, directing you through the moves toward changing troublesome feelings into open doors for self-improvement.

Rather than keeping away from or smothering feelings, you'll figure out how to embrace them as impetus for good change.

Mindfulness, self-compassion, and reframing techniques are all incorporated into this section's practical emotional alchemy strategies. By taking part in this catalytic cycle, you'll find the strength that emerges from confronting and changing testing feelings. " Nervous About Nothing" turns into your friend in this catalytic excursion, enabling you to rise up out of personal difficulties, more grounded, smarter, and more receptive to your internal identity.

In Part Three, feelings are not viewed as simple vacillations but rather as strong powers that shape the story of your life. Riding the profound rollercoaster, understanding the gradually expanding influence, and rehearsing close to home speculative chemistry are the instruments that "Nervous About Nothing" gives to direct you through this complex close to home scene.

Imagine a future in which your feelings are not obstacles but rather stepping stones on your way to lasting well-being and emotional intelligence as you embrace these ideas.

Section Four: Dread Variable

In the domain of the brain, dread frequently remains as an imposing guard, impacting choices, molding ways of behaving, and creating shaded areas on our true capacity.

Part Four of "Nervous About Nothing" is a profound plunge into the Trepidation Variable — an excursion that urges you to defy fears head-on, change dread into fuel for self-awareness, and fabricate flexibility that endures life's difficulties.

A. Standing up to Fears Head-On:

Fears, when left ignored, can transform into shadows that obscure the edges of our brains. " Nervous About Nothing" welcomes you to go up against fears head-on, enlightening the extraordinary power that comes from confronting the wellsprings of nervousness straightforwardly.

This section guides you through a course of thoughtfulness to distinguish and figure out the foundations of your feelings of trepidation.

Useful systems, established in mental social standards, enable you to challenge and rethink dread actuating considerations. You can free yourself from anxiety's grip on your mental landscape by confronting your fears head-on. Not only will you learn how to deal with your fears, but you will also learn how to regain control over how you react to them, which will ultimately help you develop courage and resilience.

B. Changing Trepidation into Fuel:

Dread, when bridled and changed, turns into a strong impetus for self-awareness and accomplishment. " Nervous About Nothing" presents the idea of changing trepidation into fuel —a cycle that includes reexamining dread as a wellspring of inspiration and motivation.

By moving your point of view on dread, you can involve it as a main thrust toward positive change.

Take a look at real-world examples and practical exercises that will help you harness the power of fear and put it to good use.

This section will show you how to use fear as a tool for self-discovery and empowerment, whether it's pursuing personal goals, accepting challenges, or stepping outside of your comfort zone. You will discover new facets of your own potential and resilience as you turn fear into fuel.

C. Developing Resilience:

The shield that protects the mind from life's storms is resilience. The book "Nervous About Nothing" emphasizes the significance of developing resilience as a fundamental skill for overcoming fears and navigating difficulties. This part gives an exhaustive manual for versatility building strategies, drawing from mental standards, care practices, and genuine insight.

From fostering a development outlook to developing self-empathy, you'll investigate a scope of methodologies to improve your capacity to return quickly from misfortune. Flexibility isn't tied in with keeping away from troubles however about fostering the solidarity to confront them with mental fortitude and versatility. As you mesh flexibility into the texture of your attitude, dread loses its hold, and you arise more grounded even with life's vulnerabilities.

The Fear Factor is presented as a terrain that can be explored and conquered rather than an impassable obstacle in Chapter 4. Nervous About Nothing" turns into your aid in standing up to fears, changing them into wellsprings of inspiration, and building versatility that rises above nervousness. Imagine a future where dread turns into a venturing stone, driving you towards an existence of mental fortitude, development, and steadfast strength.

Section Five: Stress Less, Live More

In the buzzing about present day life, stress can turn into an unwanted buddy, affecting both our psychological and actual prosperity.

Part Five of "Nervous About Nothing" is a complete investigation of stress — an excursion that guides you through dominating pressure from the executives, embracing the craft of unwinding, and developing a peaceful outlook to open an existence of equilibrium and satisfaction.

A. Dominating Pressure The executives:

Stress is an inescapable piece of life, yet the way in which we answer it can have a significant effect. " Nervous About Nothing" acquaints you with the craft of dominating pressure on the executives, giving bits of knowledge into perceiving, understanding, and successfully exploring stressors.

This section guides you through commonsense procedures established in mental social methods, care, and using time effectively.

By distinguishing pressure sets off and carrying out proactive methods for dealing with especially difficult times, you'll oversee pressure instead of being constrained by it.

This section gives you the tools to build a mindset that resists stress, from setting goals that are attainable to learning how to effectively solve problems. As you face pressure from the board, you make an establishment for a stronger and healthy lifestyle.

B. The Specialty of Unwinding:

Unwinding isn't an extravagance however a fundamental part of mental and actual prosperity. " The book "Nervous About Nothing" delves into the art of relaxation and provides a collection of methods for calming the mind and body.

You'll try a variety of techniques that can be tailored to a variety of lifestyles and preferences, such as guided imagery and progressive muscle relaxation.

In the midst of the demands of daily life, this chapter emphasizes the importance of scheduling time for relaxation. You will be able to seamlessly incorporate relaxation techniques and advice into your daily life, resulting in a sense of calm and renewal. You will realize the transformative power of intentional rest as you embrace the art of relaxation and let go of stress.

C. Making a Peaceful Mentality:

The psyche's scene can be a peaceful desert spring even amidst life's tempests. " Nervous About Nothing" guides you in making a quiet outlook — a psychological safe-haven where stress holds little influence.

 This section gives you the tools to develop a mindset that fosters peace, gratitude, and resilience by examining the fundamentals of mindfulness and positive psychology.

You will develop a sense of serenity by learning to anchor your awareness in the present moment through mindfulness and gratitude exercises.

Positive confirmations and mental rethinking methods become instruments for reshaping your viewpoint and supporting a serene outlook. Stress subsides rather than worsens as you incorporate these techniques into your daily routine.

In Section Five, "Nervous About Nothing" turns into your sidekick chasing a pressure safe and satisfying life.

Dominating pressure from the executives, embracing the specialty of unwinding, and making a quiet outlook are not far off beliefs but rather reasonable methodologies that engage you to live more completely.

Imagine a future where stress turns into a reasonable buddy, and every day unfurls with a feeling of quietness, balance, and reestablished energy.

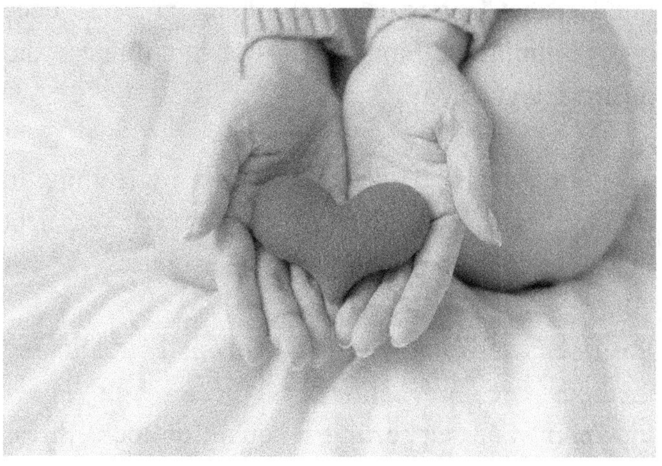

Section Six: The profound Mind-Body Connection

The interplay between the mind and body is a symphony that influences every aspect of our lives in the intricate dance of well-being.

The profound Mind-Body Connection is the subject of Chapter Six of "Nervous About Nothing." It encourages you to embrace the harmony of mental and physical health, adopt holistic well-being strategies, and learn the art of fueling the brain for optimal performance.

A. The Congruity of Mental and Actual Wellbeing:

The mind and body are connected aspects of our being, not separate entities. This chapter begins by delving into the harmony between mental and physical health.

Understanding the complex correspondence between the mind and the body gives experiences into how way of life, sustenance, and exercise influence actual wellbeing as well as mental prosperity.

The foundation for a holistic approach to health is practical advice on how to incorporate movement into your daily routine, promote good sleep hygiene, and nourish your body with healthy foods. As you embrace the congruity among mental and actual wellbeing, you engage yourself to establish a climate that upholds the two parts of your prosperity.

B. All encompassing Ways to deal with Prosperity:

Prosperity reaches out past the shortfall of disease — it envelops an all encompassing perspective on wellbeing that incorporates close to home, social, and profound aspects.

" Nervous About Nothing" welcomes you to investigate all encompassing ways to deal with prosperity, perceiving the interconnected idea of different parts of your life. This part presents care rehearsals, stress decrease procedures, and techniques for developing significant associations.

You will discover that well-being is not a destination but rather an ongoing journey that involves balance and integration if you adopt a holistic perspective. Genuine models and noteworthy advances guide you in making a balanced way to deal with wellbeing that supports your whole self. You will discover that holistic well-being becomes a strong foundation for navigating life's challenges with grace and vitality as you embrace it.

C. Powering the Cerebrum for Ideal Execution:

The mind, the war room of our being, requires appropriate sustenance to work at its ideal. " Nervous About Nothing" investigates the craft of filling the mind for ideal execution, stressing the effect of sustenance, hydration, and mental activities on smartness.

This part gives experiences into the mind stomach association, featuring the job of stomach wellbeing in impacting temperament and mental capability.

Practicing cognitive exercises, drinking enough water, and including brain-boosting foods in your diet are all good ways to keep your mind active. By understanding the advantageous connection between the cerebrum and the body, you'll figure out how to improve your way of life to help mental wellbeing. You give yourself the ability to handle the cognitive demands of life with clarity and resilience by providing your brain with the necessary fuel for peak performance.

In Section Six, "Nervous About Nothing" turns into an aide in the investigation of the Brain Body Association — an excursion that rises above the limits among mental and actual wellbeing.

Embrace the congruity of your psyche and body, take on comprehensive ways to deal with prosperity, and fuel your cerebrum for ideal execution. Imagine your well-being as a symphony of balance, resilience, and vibrant health in the future, laying the groundwork for a life of vitality and fulfillment.

Section Seven: Social Antics

Social corporations are a major part of the human experience, forming our connections, impacting our prosperity, and in some cases, introducing difficulties.

Part Seven of "Nervous About Nothing" plunges into the domain of Social Trickeries, directing you through exploring social nervousness, building significant associations, and embracing the extraordinary force of weakness.

A. Exploring Social Nervousness:

Many people face social anxiety, which can make it hard to enjoy social interactions. This chapter, "Nervous About Nothing," begins by delving into the intricacies of social anxiety and its causes and manifestations. Functional systems established in mental conduct treatment and openness methods enable you to explore social uneasiness with certainty.

This section aims to make social anxiety less of a stigma by providing a sympathetic perspective on the internal struggles that people may experience. You will acquire the tools to challenge and reframe the thoughts that contribute to social anxiety by comprehending the thought patterns that cause it. This will pave the way for more authentic and comfortable social interactions. Imagine a future where social interactions are more of an opportunity for connection than a source of anxiety as you deal with social anxiety.

B. Building Significant Associations:

The embroidery of life is woven with the strings of significant associations. "Nervous About Nothing" encourages you to embrace the art of cultivating relationships that improve your well-being and transcending superficial interactions to create meaningful connections.

Effective communication, active listening, and developing empathy—the foundations of meaningful connections—are covered in this section.

You'll learn how to navigate the complexities of social dynamics in both professional and personal relationships with real-world examples and exercises. You will realize that the quality of your interactions matters more than the quantity as you embrace the art of creating meaningful connections. These associations become a wellspring of help, bliss, and flexibility on your excursion toward a seriously satisfying life.

C. Embracing Weakness:

In reality, vulnerability, which is frequently regarded as a weakness, is a significant source of strength. Nervous About Nothing" investigates the extraordinary force of embracing weakness in friendly collaborations.

This segment difficulties cultural standards that compare weakness with delicacy, empowering you to consider it to be a fearless demonstration that cultivates credible associations.

Through private stories, activities, and reflections, you'll figure out how to embrace weakness as a door to more profound connections and self-awareness.

This part gives apparatuses to defining solid limits, communicating veritable feelings, and developing self-empathy even with weakness. As you embrace weakness, you make the way for more extravagant, more significant social associations that add to your general prosperity.

In Part Seven, "Nervous About Nothing" turns into your aid in exploring Social Trickeries — an excursion that changes social nervousness into certainty, superficial collaborations into significant associations, and weakness into strength.

Imagine a future where social collaborations become a wellspring of bliss, development, and backing, making an embroidery of connections that enhance your life.

Section Eight: Future Concentration

As we approach the finishing up section of "Nervous About Nothing," the center moves in the direction representing things to come — a future formed by mentality, assumptions, and the capacity to change difficulties into open doors.

Section Eight assists you through developing a development outlook, setting reasonable assumptions, and opening the groundbreaking capability of difficulties.

A. Developing a Development Outlook:

The focal point through which we view difficulties shapes our excursion toward self-awareness. " Nervous About Nothing" welcomes you to develop a development outlook — a viewpoint that sees difficulties not as unconquerable hindrances but rather as any open doors for learning and improvement.

This part investigates the central standards of a development mentality and gives noteworthy stages to coordinate it into your day to day routine.

You will learn to embrace the learning process, persevere in the face of setbacks, and view effort as a path to mastery through real-world examples and exercises.

Developing a development mentality isn't just about exploring difficulties; It's about cultivating a mindset that leads you toward a future filled with self-sufficiency, perseverance, and satisfaction.

B. Setting Practical Assumptions:

Assumptions, when sensible, become a compass directing us through life's vulnerabilities. " Nervous About Nothing" digs into the specialty of setting sensible assumptions, assisting you with finding some kind of harmony among aspiration and sober mindedness.

This segment gives bits of knowledge into perceiving and testing unreasonable assumptions that might add to pressure and tension.

Down to earth systems for laying out feasible objectives, overseeing hairsplitting, and fostering a sound point of view on progress engage you to explore existence with a feeling of lucidity and reason.

As you embrace the craft of setting sensible assumptions, you'll find that your process turns out to be more reasonable, and each step in the right direction turns into a festival of progress and self-awareness.

C. Transforming Difficulties into Valuable open doors:

Challenges are not road obstructions; they are venturing stones to change. Nervous About Nothing" focuses on the transformative power of transforming obstacles into opportunities.

This part directs you through reexamining your viewpoint on challenges, seeing them as impetus for development as opposed to obstructions to progress.

You'll learn how to overcome obstacles with creativity and adaptability through exercises that build resilience, solve problems, and reframe problems. You'll discover that obstacles become gateways to new possibilities and setbacks become launchpads for future success as you turn challenges into opportunities.

In Section Eight, "Nervous About Nothing" turns into a guide for your future concentration — an excursion that rises above tension and pushes you toward an eventual fate of development, strength, and satisfaction.

Develop a development outlook that sees possible challenges, set sensible assumptions that guide you with clearness, and transform difficulties into open doors that fuel your own and proficient development.

Imagine a future where each step in the right direction is met with hopefulness, where difficulties are embraced, and where your outlook turns into the compass that leads you toward an existence of direction and fulfillment.

Conclusion

When "Nervous About Nothing" comes to an end, it's not just the beginning of a new chapter. Instead, it's an invitation to embark on a never-ending journey within, exploring the complexities of your mind and discovering the transformative power that lies within you.

A. The Never-Ending Journey Inside:

The human psyche is an immense and complex scene, and the excursion inside is both a test and an open door. "Nervous About Nothing" encourages you to continue this journey with curiosity, compassion, and bravery.

The book encourages you to embrace the ever-changing nature of your mind because it recognizes that self-discovery is a process that takes a lifetime.

The endless journey within entails cultivating a mindset that welcomes growth, resilience, and a deeper understanding of oneself rather than reaching a final destination. May you find solace and empowerment in the knowledge that the journey itself is a valuable and enriching experience as you navigate the twists and turns of your own mind.

B. Nervous About Nothing: A Friend for Life:

"Nervous About Nothing" isn't simply a book; It will always be there for you as you strive for a life that is more peaceful, more enduring, and more satisfying. Every part fills in as an aide, offering bits of knowledge, commonsense methodologies, and a guide to explore the intricacies of your brain.

Whether you're confronting tension, looking for self-awareness, or essentially hoping to improve your prosperity, this book remains as a solid buddy, prepared to help you on your excursion.

"Nervous About Nothing" should serve as a source of motivation, support, and self-confidence for you as you navigate life's challenges and triumphs. Keep it inside arm's scope, getting back to its pages at whatever point you want direction, consolation, or a new viewpoint on your own psyche and your general surroundings.

C. Assets for Additional Investigation:

"Nervous About Nothing" is only the beginning of a personal journey within. In this finishing up segment, you'll find an organized rundown of assets for additional investigation. These resources, which range from recommended books and websites to guided meditation apps and online communities, are intended to work in conjunction with the ideas and methods presented in this book.

Choose the ones that best suit your requirements and preferences as you explore these resources at your own pace. The excursion inside is a cooperative exertion, and these extra instruments can offer significant help, different viewpoints, and extra strategies to upgrade your psychological prosperity.

All in all, "Nervous About Nothing" is an encouragement to embrace the wealth of your internal world, changing apprehension into strength, nervousness into an open door, and difficulties into venturing stones. On your lifetime journey within, may you find peace, purpose, and resilience at every turn, and may this book be your trusted companion.